INUIT

ABORIGINAL PEOPLES OF CANADA

Erinn Banting

Published by Weigl Educational Publishers Limited
6325 10 Street S.E.
Calgary, Alberta, Canada
T2H 2Z9

Website: www.weigl.com

Library and Archives Canada Cataloguing in Publication

Banting, Erinn, 1976-
          Inuit : Aboriginal peoples of Canada / Erinn Banting.
(Aboriginal peoples of Canada)
Includes index.
ISBN 978-1-55388-510-8 (bound).--ISBN 978-1-55388-517-7 (pbk.)
          1. Inuit--Juvenile literature. I. Title.
II. Series: Aboriginal peoples of Canada (Calgary, Alta.)
E99.E7B3553 2009   j971.9004'9712   C2009-903522-7

Printed in the United States of America
1 2 3 4 5 6 7 8 9 0 13 12 11 10 09

Photograph and Text Credits

Cover: Alamy; Alamy: pages 1, 10R, llL, llM, 15, 16, 17, 20, 21, 23; Canadian Museum of Civilization: pages 9M (IV-C-4225, D2005-10913), 9B (IV-C-4235 a-b, D2004-04609), 12B (IV-C-3498 a-b (D2003-17337), 13B (IV-C-2776, D2003-12348) ; Corbis: page 6; Getty Images: pages 4, 5, 7, 8, 9T, 10L, 11R, 12T, 13T, 14, 22.

Every reasonable effort has been made to trace ownership and to obtain permission to reprint copyright material. The publishers would be pleased to have any errors or omissions brought to their attention so that they may be corrected in subsequent printings.

All of the Internet URLs given in the book were valid at the time of publication. However, due to the dynamic nature of the Internet, some addresses may have changed, or sites may have ceased to exist since publication. While the author and publisher regret any inconvenience this may cause readers, no responsibility for any such changes can be accepted by either the author or the publisher.

We gratefully acknowledge the financial support of the Government of Canada through the Book Publishing Industry Development Program (BPIDP) for our publishing activities.

PROJECT COORDINATOR Heather Kissock

DESIGN Terry Paulhus, Kenzie Browne

ILLUSTRATOR Martha Jablonski-Jones

Contents

The People

Nearly 1,000 years ago, Inuit **ancestors** arrived in what is now Canada's Far North. They travelled hundreds of kilometres from Alaska and settled in the parts of Canada now known as Nunavut, the Northwest Territories, and northern Quebec.

In the past, the Inuit moved from one place to another during the seasons. Inuit life was based on the **migration** of animal herds, such as caribou. Since these animals were an important food source, the Inuit followed the herds wherever they went.

NET LINK

Find out more about Inuit ancestors called the Thule at **www.civilization.ca/ cmc/exhibitions/tresors/ethno/etb0320e.shtml**.

Inuit Homes

In the summer, the Inuit built tents made from wooden poles or the rib bones of whales. The poles were spread out in a circle. One end was fastened to the ground. The other end was fastened to the other poles to form a cone. The frame was then covered in animal skins.

Inuit Ideas

The Inuit filled the cracks between igloo blocks with snow. This kept wind from blowing into the building.

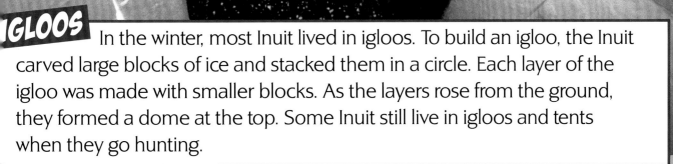

IGLOOS

In the winter, most Inuit lived in igloos. To build an igloo, the Inuit carved large blocks of ice and stacked them in a circle. Each layer of the igloo was made with smaller blocks. As the layers rose from the ground, they formed a dome at the top. Some Inuit still live in igloos and tents when they go hunting.

Inuit Clothing

PARKAS

Parkas were made from caribou hides.
Women's parkas had a special pouch
to hold small children.

PANTS

Pants often were made from caribou
hides. This protected the Inuit from
freezing wind, ice, and snow.

MITTENS

Sealskin was used to make mittens because it was strong and did not let in water.

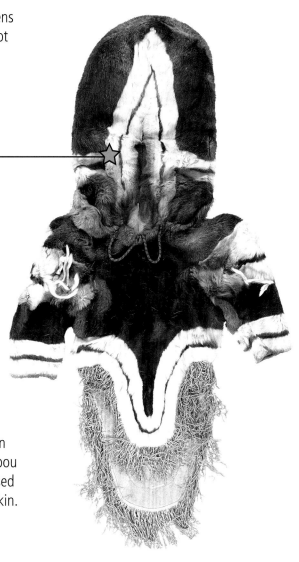

DECORATION

Many Inuit added decorations to their clothing. These decorations were made from materials found in the environment. Rabbit fur was often used to create fringes.

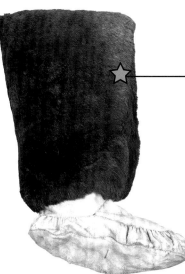

BOOTS

Inuit boots were called kamiks. Kamiks that were to be worn on land only were made from caribou skin. Kamiks that were to be used in water were made from sealskin.

Hunting and Gathering

CARIBOU

Caribou was the Inuit's main food. The Inuit ate all parts of the animal, including the fat, bones, and blood, to ensure they had the proper **nutrients**. Caribou could be dried, smoked, or salted to keep it over the long winter.

FISH

The Inuit fished in the Arctic Ocean, as well as the lakes and rivers of the North. Arctic char was one of the most common catches. This type of fish can be eaten raw, frozen, dried, or cooked.

The Inuit relied on their environment for food. They hunted and fished the animals found in the area where they lived. In the summer months, the Inuit gathered berries and other plants. The plants were then dried so that the Inuit could eat them in the winter.

NUTS AND BERRIES

Vegetables could not grow in the frozen Arctic soil. The Inuit ate nuts and berries to get the nutrients vegetables offered.

BANNOCK

Bannock is a type of bread the Inuit made. Dough was wrapped around a stick and cooked over an open fire.

PEMMICAN

Pemmican was made from meat, animal fat, and berries. They were mixed together and then dried or stored in containers.

Inuit Tools

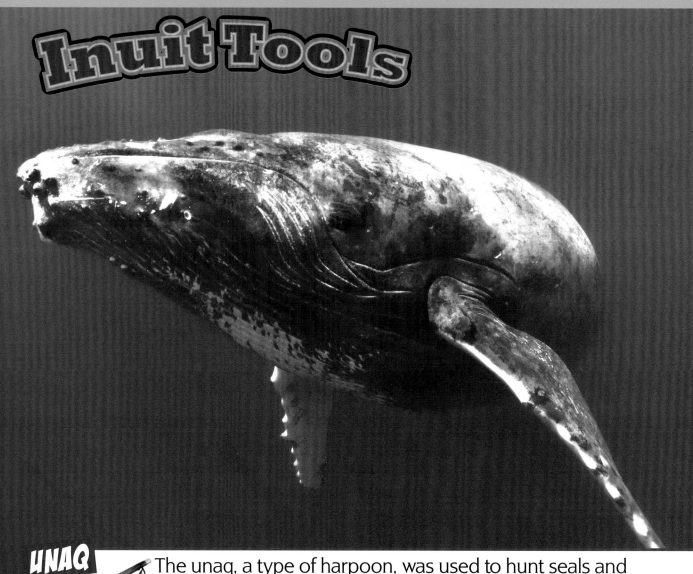

UNAQ The unaq, a type of harpoon, was used to hunt seals and whales. One end of the harpoon was connected to a rope. Hunters used the rope to pull the animal toward them.

Inuit Ideas

To protect their eyes from the Sun, the Inuit wore wooden goggles that had thin slits. The Inuit could see through the slits, and less sunlight reached their eyes.

NITSIQ

A tool called a nitsiq was used to pull animals from the water. The nitsiq had a sharp hook on the end of its handle. The hook was used to pull harpooned animals out of the water.

Moving from Place to Place

KOMATIKS Since the Inuit hunted and followed herds, they sometimes had to travel long distances. Sleds called komatiks were pulled by one or more dogs. The sleds were used to carry people, supplies, and animals across the land.

KAYAKS AND UMIAKS

Water travel was important to the Inuit. Kayaks were used for hunting and fishing. The Inuit used umiaks to move people and goods from site to site. These boats were larger and deeper than kayaks. Both boats were made by stretching animal skins over a frame made from wood or animal bones. Today, most Inuit use snowmobiles and motorboats to travel from one place to another.

Inuit Music and Dance

Drum dancing is an important part of Inuit **culture**. To begin a drum dance, a group of singers form a circle and begin singing. A dancer then picks up a drum and enters the circle. Dancers drum while they dance.

The Inuit are known for their throat singing. When throat singing, two people face each other and sing a series of sounds. Some are meant to sound like animals. The singers work together to make unique sounds with their voices.

NET LINK
To listen to Inuit throat singing, surf over to www.youtube.com/watch?v=jmzm9VEsazI.

The Story of Nuliajuk

Nuliajuk was one of the most powerful spirits worshipped by the Inuit. She was believed to be the mother of all sea creatures.

When Nuliajuk was old enough, she married what she thought was a man. However, she soon discovered that her husband was a bird that had disguised itself as a man. Nuliajuk tried to escape her husband by boat, but he caught her and turned over her boat with his large wings.

As she fell into the sea, Nuliajuk lost her fingers. They became the many creatures that call the waters home.

Inuit Art

The Inuit are well known for their sculptures. Most Inuit sculptures are made from stone found in the Far North. Bones and ivory are also used. Inuit sculptures are often carved in the form of people and animals.

To give their sculptures a glossy finish, the Inuit rub melted beeswax over their creation.

Art prints are another form of Inuit art. Prints are made by carving a design into a piece of stone or bone. The prints often show scenes from the Inuit's daily life.

Make Your Own Bannock

Ingredients
  4 cups flour
  0.5 teaspoons salt
  1.5 tablespoons baking powder
  1.5 cups water

Equipment
  A large mixing bowl
  Measuring cups
  A baking pan

1. Mix all of the ingredients together in a large bowl.
2. Sprinkle flour on a flat, clean surface, and knead the dough.
3. Roll the dough into a loaf.
4. With an adult's help, bake for 30 minutes at 350 degrees Fahrenheit.
5. Serve with jam or honey.

Glossary

ancestors: people who lived in the past

culture: the arts, beliefs, and habits that make up a community, people, or country

migration: to move from one place to another

nutrients: substances that nourish a living creature